SKILL BUILDING FOR ESL
AND SPECIAL EDUCATION

SIMPLY ENGLISH SERIES

Simply English is an ESL curriculum adaptable for elementary though adult learners. Its goal is to help the limited and/or non-English speaker achieve fluency in English words that are essential for everyday life. Simply English can also be incorporated into special education programs for students who need help with spelling, definitions of words, and correct application of grammatical structures. The forty-four instructional units contain the basic information that ELS and special education students need to function independently.

Books in the Series:

Skill Building for ESL and Special Education: Teacher's Text
Skill Building for ESL and Special Education: Student Workbook
Skill Building for ESL and Special Education: Student Textbook

LDING FOR ESL
AND SPECIAL EDUCATION

Student Workbook

Kristine Setting Clark

Rowman & Littlefield
Lanham • Boulder • New York • London

Published by Rowman & Littlefield
A wholly owned subsidary of The Rowman & Littlefield Publishing Group, Inc.
4501 Forbes Boulevard, Suite 200, Lanham, Maryland 20706
www.rowman.com

Unit A, Whitacre Mews, 26-34 Stannary Street, London SE11 4AB

British Library Cataloguing in Publication Information Available

Library of Congress Cataloging-in-Publication Data Available

978-1-4758-2630-2 (paper)
978-1-4758-2631-9 (ebook)

∞™ The paper used in this publication meets the minimum requirements of American National Standard for Information Sciences—Permanence of Paper for Printed Library Materials, ANSI/NISO Z39.48-1992.

Printed in the United States of America

Contents

Introduction

The *Simply English Student Workbook* will help you to develop a vocabulary of practical words, phrases, and slang that you will use in everyday situations with English speakers within the United States. The forty-four units in this workbook parallel the same numbered units in the *Simply English Student Textbook*.

The *Simply English Student Workbook and Simply English Student Textbook* is a new approach—a topical approach—different from the traditional style of learning a new language. It is different because you will have the opportunity to practice your skills in reading, writing, listening, and speaking. This, in turn, will help you to develop more confidence in self-expression.

A *Personal History Form* is included to help you organize important information when applying for college and the job market.

Each of the forty-four units in the *Simply English Student Workbook* contain contains the following material:

Dialogue: Each unit of the workbook begins with a *situational dialogue* (the first being on page 5). The characters in these *skits* go to the restaurant, to school, to the doctor, to the dentist, and so on. They have hobbies both indoor and outdoor, go shopping at the supermarket and department store, and even learn about money and banking.

The dialogues are long enough to allow situations to develop *naturally* to create a real-life conversational pattern. Bu incorporating the structures of the corresponding unit within the text, you will be given a great deal of practice in reading and an even greater chance of comprehension.

First you should study the dialogue. Next, read it aloud with a partner, and finally portray the characters by reading and acting out the dialogue in front of the class.

Dialogue Completion: Here you will progress from an understanding of the dialogue vocabulary to the comprehension of how the vocabulary and structures are used and applied in conversation. In this activity you will be asked to complete, first verbally and then in writing, the blank part(s) of the conversation. This will be found on the second page of each unit (for example, see page 6).

Class Activities: The class activities (shown on the next page) are designed to involve either small groups or the entire class in using what you have learned in the unit(s) previously taught. Posters and/or pictures of situations that parallel the unit are good *learning tools* for expansion and development of the English language. As you progress and gain confidence in your new language, *skits* can be created and performed in front of the class.

The following are instructions for class activities:

1. Get into small groups, each time trading roles according to the dialogue.

2. Change the names of the characters and where they are from, what they are doing, where they are going, what they are buying, and so on, in accordance with the dialogue material.

3. Make additions or deletions to the dialogue. This can be made easier or more complex depending upon your progress.

4. Using the model, make up your own dialogue and use the vocabulary from your corresponding text to help you.

5. Skits (using various props) can be performed in front of the class.

PERSONAL HISTORY

Name_____

       Last   First   Middle

Address_____

      Number   Street

City_____**State**_____

Telephone_____   _____

           Home   Cell

Email_____

Age_____**Height**_____**Weight**_____

          Feet/Inches   Pounds

Color of Eyes_____**Color of Hair**_____

Date of Birth_____

         Month   Day   Year

Place of Birth_____

Highest School Grade Completed: 7 8 9 10 11 12

University Attended_____

Degrees_____

Social Security #_____

Marital Status: Single___Married___Separated___Divorced__

Father's Name_____

Father's Birthplace_____

Mother's Name_____

Mother's Birthplace_____

1

Personal Identification I

MARIA	Hello, Bill. How are you?
BILL	I'm fine. How are you, Maria?
MARIA	Fine, thank you. I'd like to introduce my friend, Sylvia.
BILL	Hi, Sylvia. I'm very glad to meet you.
SYLVIA	Nice to meet you, Bill.
BILL	Where are you from, Sylvia?
SYLVIA	I'm from San Francisco, California.
MARIA	Sylvia and I have to leave now.
SYLVIA	It was a pleasure to meet you, Bill.

MARIA   Hello, Bill. How are you?

BILL   _____

MARIA   I'd like to _____ my friend, Sylvia.

BILL   _____

SYLVIA   I'm from San Francisco, California.

MARIA   Sylvia and I have to leave now.

SYLVIA   It was a pleasure to meet you, Bill.

BILL   _____

       _____

MARIA & SYLVIA Bye, Bill.

2

Personal Identification II

TEACHER	Hello. What is your name?
STUDENT	My name is Justin Mendez.
TEACHER	What is your address, Justin?
STUDENT	My address is 2170 30th Avenue, San Francisco, California.
TEACHER	What is your phone number?
STUDENT	My phone number is 555-495-4449.
TEACHER	Where were you born?
STUDENT	I was born in Monterrey, Mexico.
TEACHER	What is your birthdate?
STUDENT	My birthdate is October 23, 2005.
TEACHER	How old are you?
STUDENT	I am ten years old.
TEACHER	Do you have any brothers or sisters?
STUDENT	Yes. I have three brothers.
TEACHER	What language do you speak at home?
STUDENT	I speak Spanish with my parents and English with my brothers.
TEACHER	What are your parents' names?
STUDENT	Their names are Mario and Maribel Mendez.
TEACHER	Who should I call in case of an emergency?
STUDENT	You can call my mother. Her home phone number is 555-595-4449, her cell number is 555-516-9999 and her business number is 555-897-1111.
TEACHER	Thank you very much, Justin.
STUDENT	You're welcome.

TEACHER   Hello. What's your name?

STUDENT   _____

TEACHER   What is your address?

STUDENT   _____

TEACHER   What is your phone number?

STUDENT   _____

TEACHER   Where were you born?

STUDENT   _____

TEACHER   What is your birthdate?

STUDENT   _____

TEACHER   How old are you?

STUDENT   _____

TEACHER   Do you have any brothers or sisters?

STUDENT   _____

TEACHER   What language do you speak at home?

STUDENT   _____

                   _____

TEACHER   What are your parents' names?

STUDENT   _____

TEACHER   Who should I call in case of an emergency?

STUDENT   _____

                   _____

TEACHER   Thank you very much.

STUDENT   You're welcome.

3

Education and Schooling I

DAVID	Hi, Susan. How are you today?
SUSAN	I'm fine, thanks. How are you?
DAVID	I'm fine.
SUSAN	This is such a nice school. I really like it.
DAVID	Where did you attend school last year?
SUSAN	I attended school in Paris, France.
DAVID	What grade were you in last year?
SUSAN	I was in the ninth grade.
DAVID	What classes are you taking this semester?
SUSAN	I am taking classes in math, history, science, ESL, art and physical education. What is your schedule this semester?
DAVID	I am taking ESL, wood shop, computers, American history, physical education, and science.
SUSAN	Do you like all your teachers?
DAVID	Yes. They are all very nice.
SUSAN	I like all of my teachers, too.
DAVID	I have to go to class now. Bye, Susan.
SUSAN	Bye, David. See you later.

DAVID   Hi, Susan. How are you today?

SUSAN   _____

DAVID   I'm fine.

SUSAN   This is such a nice school. I really like it.

DAVID   _____

SUSAN   I attended school in Paris, France.

DAVID   _____

SUSAN   I was in the ninth grade.

DAVID   _____

SUSAN   I am taking classes in math, history, science, ESL, art, and physical education. What is your schedule this semester?

DAVID   _____

                       _____

SUSAN   Do you like all of your teachers?

DAVID   _____

SUSAN   I like all of my teachers, too.

DAVID   _____

SUSAN   Bye, David. See you later.

4

Education and Schooling II

SUSAN	Excuse me. Where is Room 203?
ROBERT	It's in the building behind the gym.
SUSAN	Thank you.

(Susan sees Jeannine.)

SUSAN	Hi, Jeannine.
JEANNINE	Hi, Susan.
SUSAN	I want to change my schedule. I have to add a class.
JEANNINE	Do you have enough credits to graduate?
SUSAN	I think so.
JEANNINE	You should talk to your counselor.
SUSAN	I will. Thank you. Good-bye.

(Susan sees Steve.)

SUSAN	Hi, Steve.
STEVE	Hi, Susan.
SUSAN	Do you know what time it is?
STEVE	It is 10:55.
SUSAN	I have to go. I don't want to be late for my English class.
STEVE	Bye, Susan.
SUSAN	Bye.

SUSAN	Excuse me. Where is _____?
ROBERT	_____
SUSAN	_____
ROBERT	You're welcome.

(Susan sees Jeannine.)

SUSAN	Hi, Jeannine.
JEANNINE	Hi, Susan.
SUSAN	I want to change my schedule. I have to _____.
JEANNINE	Do you have enough credits to graduate?
SUSAN	_____
JEANNINE	You should talk to your counselor.
SUSAN	I will. Thank you. Good-bye.
JEANNINE	Good-bye.

(Susan sees Steve.)

SUSAN	Hi, Steve.
STEVE	Hi, Susan.
SUSAN	Do you know what time it is?
STEVE	_____
SUSAN	I have to go. I don't want to be late for _____.
	_____
STEVE	Bye, Susan.
SUSAN	Bye.

5

The Telephone/The Cell Phone

JOEY	I just bought a new smartphone today.
BILLY	What kind of phone is it and what features does it have?
JOEY	I bought an iPhone and it has email, texting, photos, video, GPS (Global Positioning System), and much more.
BILLY	Wow! That sounds great!
JOEY	I think I'll try out my phone and call my sister in San Francisco.

(Joey calls his sister, Gina.)

GINA	Hello.
JOEY	Hi, Gina. I am calling you from my new smartphone.
GINA	That's great. Was it difficult to learn how to use it?
JOEY	No, not at all. The salesperson at the store showed me how to use it.
GINA	I really need to buy a smartphone. I am still using my cordless phone at home and sometimes I have dropped calls.
JOEY	I have very few dropped calls with my cell phone. Well, I have to go now. Hope to see you soon.
GINA	I think I will go shopping tomorrow and see about buying a smartphone. It was great talking to you.
JOEY	Great talking to you, too. Bye, Gina.

JOEY   _____

BILLY   What kind of phone is it and what features does it have?

JOEY   _____

     _____

     _____

BILLY   Wow! That sounds great!

JOEY   _____

(Joey calls his sister, Gina.)

GINA   Hello.

JOEY   Hi, Gina. I am calling you from my new smartphone.

GINA   _____

JOEY   No, not at all. The salesperson at the store showed me how to use it.

GINA   _____

     _____

     _____

JOEY   I have very few dropped calls with my cell phone. Well, I have to go now. Hope to see you soon.

GINA   _____

     _____

JOEY   Great talking to you, too. Bye, Gina.

6

Behavior

BRIAN	Could you please loan me your pencil?
DENISE	Sure. Here you are.

(Brian and the cashier)

BRIAN	Could I please have change for a dollar?
CASHIER	Sure. How would you like it?
BRIAN	I would like three quarters, two dimes, and a nickel.
CASHIER	Here you are.
BRIAN	Thanks.

(Brian and Michelle.)

BRIAN	I'm having a party at my house this weekend. Would you like to come?
MICHELLE	Sure. I would love to.
BRIAN	Great! I'll tell you more about it at lunch. Bye, Michelle.
MICHELLE	Bye. Brian. See you at lunch.

(Brian and Andy)

BRIAN	Could you please turn down your radio? It's too loud!
ANDY	I'm sorry. I didn't realize it was so loud.

(Brian and Sandy)

BRIAN	I'm really sorry I broke your notebook.
SANDY	That's OK. I've got another one.
BRIAN	Well, I'll buy you another one anyway.

BRIAN   Could you please loan me your pencil?

DENISE   _____

BRIAN   Thank you.

(Brian and the cashier)

BRIAN   Could I please have _____?

CASHIER   Sure. How would you like it?

BRIAN   I would like _____

CASHIER   Here you are.

BRIAN   Thanks.

(Brian and Michelle)

BRIAN   I'm having a party at my house this weekend? Would you like to come?

MICHELLE   _____

BRIAN   Great! I'll tell you more about it at lunch. Bye, Michelle.

MICHELLE   _____

(Brian and Andy)

BRIAN   Could you please turn down your radio? It's too loud!

ANDY   _____

(Brian and Sandy)

BRIAN   I'm really sorry I broke your notebook.

SANDY   _____

BRIAN   Well, I'll buy you another one anyway.

7

Family Relationships

CAROL	Do you have any brothers or sisters?
GINA	Yes, I have three brothers and one sister.
CAROL	Are your brothers older than you?
GINA	Two are older and one is younger.
CAROL	How old is your sister?
GINA	My sister is ten. She is the same age as I am. We are twins.
CAROL	Do you have a lot of relatives?
GINA	Yes. I have about twenty or more relatives. I am making a family tree for my class. It will be made of pictures of my family.
	Do you have many relatives?
CAROL	Yes. I have four brothers, four sisters, three nieces, two nephews, two aunts, two uncles, and five cousins.
GINA	That is a big family! Why don't you make a family tree, too?
CAROL	OK. Let's make our own family trees together!

CAROL   _____

GINA   Yes. I have three brothers and one sister.

CAROL   Are your brothers older than you?

GINA   _____

CAROL   _____

GINA   My sister is ten. She is the same age as I am. We are twins.

CAROL   Do you have a lot of relatives?

GINA   _____

_____

_____

_____

Do you have many relatives?

CAROL   _____

_____

_____

GINA   That is a big family! Why don't you make a family tree, too?

CAROL   OK. Let's make our own family trees together!

8

Occupations

BILL	What do you do for a living?
KRIS	I'm a teacher. I teach Physical Education, English, and Spanish.
	What do you do?
BILL	I'm a fireman in San Francisco. I'm at Station 3.
KRIS	Is your son a fireman, too?
BILL	No, he's a mechanic.
KRIS	What does your daughter do?
BILL	My daughter is a nurse in Los Angeles and works at a local hospital.
KRIS	Well, I have to be going now. It was nice talking to you. I hope to see you soon.
BILL	Thanks. I hope to see you soon, too.

BILL   What do you do for a living?

KRIS   _____

_____

KRIS (cont.)   _____

BILL   I'm a fireman in San Francisco. I'm at Station 3.

KRIS   Is your son a fireman, too?

BILL   _____

KRIS   What does your daughter do?

BILL   _____

_____

KRIS   Well, I have to be going now. It was nice talking to you. I hope to see you soon.

BILL   _____

9

Health I

Parts of the Body

LINDA	What color are Jill's eyes?
BOB	Jill's eyes are blue.
LINDA	What color is her hair?
BOB	Her hair is brown.
LINDA	Did you see the color of her fingernails?
BOB	Yes. They were painted purple!
LINDA	Did you see the color of her toenails?
BOB	No. What color were they?
LINDA	They were green!
BOB	What happened to Jill's husband, Jim?
LINDA	Jim broke his right arm, his hip, his left leg, two of his fingers, and one of his toes. He fell down the stairs at work.
BOB	Is he going to be OK?
LINDA	He's better, but he has to stay home for the next six weeks. Jill is going to have to help him until the casts are off.

LINDA	What color are Jill's eyes?
BOB	_____!
LINDA	What color is her _____?
BOB	_____
LINDA	Did you see the color of her _____?
BOB	Yes. They were _____!
LINDA	Did you see the color of her _____?
BOB	No. What color were they?
LINDA	They were _____!
BOB	What happened to Jill's husband, Jim?
LINDA	_____
	_____
	_____
	_____
BOB	Is he going to be OK?
LINDA	_____
	_____
	_____
	_____

10

Health II

Ailments and Accidents

JILL	David, how do you feel today?
DAVID	I feel sick. My stomach and my head hurt.
JILL	Do you ache all over?
DAVID	Yes. I think I have the flu.
JILL	I am going to give you some medicine. You better stay in bed and rest.
DAVID	I will. Can you bring me something to drink? I'm very thirsty.
JILL	Sure. What would you like?
DAVID	A cup of tea and a glass of orange juice, please.
JILL	Sure. I'll get it for you right now.
DAVID	Thank you.

JILL	David, how do you feel today?
DAVID	_____
JILL	Do you ache all over?
DAVID	_____
JILL	I am going to give you some medicine. You better stay in bed and rest.
DAVID	I will. Can you bring me something to drink? I'm very thirsty.
JILL	_____
DAVID	_____
	_____
JILL	Sure. I'll get it for you right now.
DAVID	Thank you.

11

Health III

The Doctor/The Hospital

RICH	What seems to be the problem?
STEVE	I feel very sick.
RICH	You have spots all over your face! I think you have the measles!
STEVE	Maybe I should take my temperature. I feel very warm.

(Steve takes his temperature.)

STEVE	It's 102! I'm going to call the doctor. He will tell us what to do.

(Steve calls the doctor.)

NURSE	Hello, Dr. White's office. Can I help you?
STEVE	Hello. I need to make an appointment with Dr. White.
NURSE	What is the matter?
STEVE	I think I have the measles and my temperature is 102.
NURSE	Can I have your name, please?
STEVE	Steve Smith.
NURSE	We can see you at 1:00 today, Mr. Smith.
STEVE	Thank you very much. See you at 1:00.

RICH	What seems to be the problem?
STEVE	_____
RICH	You have spots all over your face! I think you have the
	_____!
STEVE	Maybe I should take my _____
	I feel very _____

(Steve takes his temperature.)

| STEVE | It's 102! I'm going to call the doctor. He will tell us what to do. |

(Steve calls the doctor.)

NURSE	_____
STEVE	Hello. I need to make an appointment with Dr. White.
NURSE	What is the matter?
STEVE	_____
NURSE	Can I have your name, please?
STEVE	_____
NURSE	We can see you at 1:00 today, Mr. Smith.
STEVE	Thank you very much. See you at 1:00.

12

Health IV

The Drugstore

LISA	I'd like to have this prescription filled. Can you fill it for me?
PHARMACIST	Yes. We have this medicine here. It comes in liquid and tablet forms. Which one would you prefer?
LISA	I would like the tablets, please.
PHARMACIST	Your order will be ready in about half an hour.
LISA	I need to get a few items here at the store. I'll be back in half an hour. Thank you.
PHARMACIST	You're welcome.

(Lisa gets a shopping basket. She puts a toothbrush, toothpaste, shampoo, and dental floss inside the basket. She returns to the pharmacy to pick up her medicine and to pay for the items.)

LISA	Is my prescription ready?
PHARMACIST	Yes. Here you are. You can pay for everything here.

(Pharmacist rings up the total.)

PHARMACIST.	That will be a total of $21.50.
LISA	Here you are. (She hands him the money.)
PHARMACIST	Thank you and have a nice day.

LISA	I'd like to have this prescription filled. Can you fill it for me?
PHARMACIST	_____
	_____
LISA	I would like the tablets, please.
PHARMACIST	_____
LISA	I need to get a few items here at the store. I'll be back in half an hour. Thank you.
PHARMACIST	You're welcome.

(Lisa gets a shopping basket. She puts a toothbrush, toothpaste, shampoo, and dental floss inside the basket. She returns to the pharmacy to pick up her medicine and to pay for the items.)

LISA	_____
PHARMACIST	Yes. Here you are. You can pay for everything here.

(Pharmacist rings up the total.)

PHARMACIST	That will be a total of _____
LISA	Here you are. (She hands him the money.)
PHARMACIST	Thank you and have a nice day.

13

Health V

The Dentist

TONY	My tooth hurts. I think I have a cavity.
KATHY	You need to go to the dentist. Do you want me to make an appointment for you?
TONY	Yes. Try to make it for today.

(Kathy calls the dentist.)

NURSE	Hello, Dr. Long's office. Can I help you?
KATHY	Hello. I need to make an appointment with Dr. Long.
NURSE	What seems to be the problem?
KATHY	My husband has a bad toothache. Could he make an appointment for today?
NURSE.	Let's see. Can he come in at 4:00 today?
KATHY	Yes. That will be fine.
NURSE	Can I have his name please?
KATHY	Tony Fazio.
NURSE	OK. The doctor will see Mr. Fazio at 4:00 today.
KATHY	Thank you.

TONY   My tooth hurts. I think I have a _____.

KATHY   _____

                          _____

TONY   Yes. Try to make it for today.

(Kathy calls the dentist.)

NURSE   Hello, Dr. Long's office. Can I help you?

KATHY   _____

                          _____

NURSE   What seems to be the problem?

KATHY   _____

                          _____

                          _____

NURSE   Let's see. Can he come in at 4:00 today?

KATHY   _____

NURSE   Can I have his name please?

KATHY   _____

NURSE   OK. The doctor will see Mr. Fazio at 4:00 today.

KATHY   Thank you.

14

Health VI

Personal Hygiene

MOTHER	Please take a shower and brush your teeth before you go to bed.
SON	I took a shower yesterday. Do I have to take another shower today?
MOTHER	Yes! You've been playing football all day. You're dirty! Wash your hair, too. You'll find the shampoo and conditioner in the shower.

(Son showers and gets ready for bed.)

MOTHER	Did you remember to brush your teeth?
SON	No, I forgot. I'll brush them now.
SON (cont.)	Mom, my gym clothes are dirty. Could you please wash them for me?
MOTHER	Yes. Put them in the washer and I'll wash them tonight.
SON	Thanks, Mom.
MOTHER	You're welcome. Good night.

MOTHER   Please take a shower and brush your teeth before you go to bed.

SON   I took a shower yesterday. Do I have to take another shower today?

MOTHER   _____

        _____

        _____

        _____

(Son showers and gets ready for bed.)

MOTHER   Did you remember to _____?

SON   No, I forgot. I'll _____.

SON (cont.)   Mom, my gym clothes are dirty. Could you please wash them for me?

MOTHER   _____

        _____

SON   Thanks, Mom.

MOTHER   You're welcome. Good night.

15

Health VII

Emergency Services

BRIAN	Brittany! Call 911! Our house is on fire!

(Brittany calls the emergency phone number, 911.)

911 EMERGENCY	What is your emergency?
BRITTANY	Help! There is a fire at 2170 30th Avenue. Please send the fire department immediately!
911 EMERGENCY	Please give me your name and phone number.
BRITTANY	My name is Brittany Clark and my phone number is 555-897-8121. Please hurry!
911 EMERGENCY	The firefighters will be there in a few minutes. Make sure everyone gets out of the house immediately.
BRITTANY	Yes, I will. Thank you.
BRITTANY	Brian! Wait outside for the fire department. It's too dangerous to stay in the house!

(Brian and Brittany immediately leave the house and wait for the fire department to arrive.)

BRIAN   Brittany! Call 911! Our house is on fire!

(Brittany calls the emergency phone number, 911.)

911 EMERGENCY What is your emergency?

BRITTANY   _____

        _____

911 EMERGENCY Please give me your name and phone number.

BRITTANY   _____

        _____

911 EMERGENCY The firefighters will be there in a few minutes. Make sure everyone gets out of the house immediately.

BRITTANY   Yes, I will. Thank you.

BRITTANY   Brian! Wait _____.

        It's too _____ to stay in the house!

(Brian and Brittany immediately leave the house and wait for the fire department to arrive.)

16

Money and Banking

JUSTIN	I'd like to deposit money into my savings account.
BANK TELLER	How much would you like to deposit?
JUSTIN	$1,000.
BANK TELLER	I will need for you to swipe your ATM card and enter your four-digit security code.

(Justin swipes his ATM card and enters his four-digit security code.)

BANK TELLER	Here's your receipt. $1,000 has been deposited into your savings account. Would you like to make another transaction?
JUSTIN	Yes. Please withdraw $250 out of my checking account.
BANK TELLER	Here you are.

(The teller counts out the money.)

JUSTIN	Thank you.
BANK TELLER	You're welcome.

JUSTIN	I'd like to deposit _____ into my savings _____.
BANK TELLER	How much would you like to deposit?
JUSTIN	_____
BANK TELLER	I will need for you to swipe your ATM card and enter your four-digit security code.

(Justin swipes his ATM card and enters his four-digit security code.)

BANK TELLER	Here's your receipt. $1,000 has been deposited into your savings account. Would you like to make another transaction?
JUSTIN	_____
	_____
BANK TELLER	_____

(The teller counts out the money.)

JUSTIN	Thank you.
BANK TELLER	You're welcome.

17

Shopping I

General

SALESPERSON	May I help you?
MARIA	Yes. I'm looking for a black dress. Could you tell me where I can find the dress department?
SALESPERSON	Yes. Follow me. It's right over here.
MARIA	These dresses are very expensive. Do you have some that are less expensive?
SALESPERSON	We have some dresses over here that are on sale.

(Maria looks through the dresses that are on sale.)

MARIA	This dress is a bargain! I'll take it!
SALESPERSON	Will that be cash, check, or credit card?
MARIA	I'll pay with cash.
SALESPERSON	Your total is $25.63.
MARIA	Here you are.

(Maria hands the clerk the money.)

SALESPERSON	Thank you for shopping with us. Come back soon.
MARIA	Good-bye.

SALESPERSON	May I help you?
MARIA	_____
	_____
	_____

SALESPERSON	Yes. Follow me. It's right over here.
MARIA	These dresses are very _____. Do you have some that are _____?
SALESPERSON	We have some dresses over here that are _____

(Maria looks through the dresses that are on sale.)

MARIA	This dress is a _____! I'll take it!
SALESPERSON	Will that be _____?
MARIA	I'll pay with cash.
SALESPERSON	Your total is _____.
MARIA	Here you are.

(Maria hands the clerk the money.)

SALESPERSON	_____
	_____
MARIA	Good-bye.

18

Shopping II
Clothing

SALESPERSON	May I help you?
RYAN	Yes, please. I'd like to try on some sweatpants.
SALESPERSON	What size do you wear?
RYAN	I wear a medium.
SALESPERSON	The medium sweatpants are on this rack. What color are you looking for?
RYAN	Grey.
SALESPERSON	Here you are. The dressing room is to the left of the cashier.

(Ryan tries on the sweatpants.)

RYAN	They fit perfectly.
SALESPERSON	Will this be cash, check, or credit card?
RYAN	I'll put it on my credit card.

(The salesperson swipes the credit card and hands it back to Ryan.)

SALESPERSON	Here's your receipt. Please sign here.

(Ryan signs the slip and returns it to the salesperson.)

SALESPERSON	Thank you. I hope you enjoy the sweatpants.
RYAN	Good-bye.

SALESPERSON   _____?

RYAN   Yes, please. I'd like to try on some _____.

SALESPERSON   _____?

RYAN   I wear a medium.

SALESPERSON   The medium sweatpants are on this rack. What color are you looking for?

RYAN   _____

SALESPERSON   Here you are. The dressing room is to the left of the cashier.

(Ryan tries on the sweatpants.)

RYAN   They fit perfectly.

SALESPERSON   _____?

RYAN   I'll put it on my credit card.

(The salesperson swipes the credit card and hands it back to Ryan.)

SALESPERSON   Here's your receipt. Please sign here.

(Ryan signs the slip and returns it to the salesperson.)

SALESPERSON   Thank you. I hope you enjoy the _____.

RYAN   Good-bye.

19

Shopping III

Accessories

SALESPERSON	Would you like to see these earrings?
GINA	Yes. They are beautiful! How much are they?
SALESPERSON	They are $80.00.
GINA	That seems a little expensive to me.
SALESPERSON	Yes, I know. But they are made of sterling silver.
GINA	Could I please see the earrings that are over here?
SALESPERSON	Of course.

(The salesperson takes the earrings out of the display case and gives them to Gina.)

SALESPERSON	Here you are.
GINA	These are also very pretty. How much are they?
SALESPERSON	They are $50.
GINA	I'll take them.
SALESPERSON	Cash, check, or credit card?
GINA	Check.
SALESPERSON	May I see your identification?

(Gina shows the salesperson her identification. The salesperson completes the transaction and gives the receipt to Gina.)

SALESPERSON	Here you are. Thank you and enjoy the earrings.
GINA	Thank you and good-bye.

SALESPERSON	Would you like to see these earrings?
GINA	_____ _____?
SALESPERSON	They are $80.
GINA	_____.
SALESPERSON	Yes, I know. But they are _____.
GINA	Could I please see the earrings that are over here?
SALESPERSON	Of course.

(The salesperson takes the earrings out of the display case and gives them to Gina.)

SALESPERSON	Here you are.
GINA	_____ _____?
SALESPERSON	They are _____.
GINA	I'll take them.
SALESPERSON	Cash, check, or credit card?
GINA	_____
SALESPERSON	May I see your identification?

(Gina shows the salesperson her identification. The salesperson completes the transaction and gives the receipt to Gina.)

SALESPERSON	Here you are. Thank you and enjoy the earrings.
GINA	Thank you and good-bye.

20

Shopping IV

The Supermarket

LISA	I need to pick up a few things at the grocery store.
MELANIE	What do you need?
LISA	I need milk, eggs, bread, butter, coffee, and chicken.
MELANIE	You should make a list of what you need so you don't forget anything.
LISA	I will.

(At the Supermarket)

LISA	Excuse me. Where can I find the coffee?
CLERK	It's in Aisle 5A.
LISA	Thanks.

(At the Meat Department)

LISA	What is the price of chicken today?
BUTCHER	It's $2.99 a pound.
LISA	I'd like two pounds, please.
BUTCHER	That will be a total of $5.98.

(The butcher hands Lisa the wrapped chicken.)

BUTCHER	Please pay the cashier at the checkout.
LISA	Thank you.

(At the checkout)

LISA	Here are my coupons.
CASHIER	Your total is $31.50. Your coupons total $2.50. You owe $29.00.
LISA	Here you are.

(Lisa hands the cashier $30.00.)

CASHIER	Here is your dollar in change. Thank you and have a nice day.

LISA	I need to pick up a few things at the grocery store.
MELANIE	What do you need?
LISA	_____
MELANIE	You should make _____ of what you need so you don't forget anything.
LISA	I will.

(At the Supermarket)

LISA	Excuse me. Where can I find the coffee?
CLERK	It's in _____.
LISA	Thanks.

(At the Meat Department)

LISA	What is the price of chicken today?
BUTCHER	It's $2.99 a pound.
LISA	I'd like _____, please.
BUTCHER	That will be a total of $5.98.

(The butcher hands Lisa the wrapped chicken.)

BUTCHER	Please pay the _____ at the checkout.
LISA	Thank you.

(At the checkout)

LISA	Here are my coupons.
CASHIER	Your total is $31.50. Your coupons total $2.50. You owe _____.
LISA	Here you are. (Lisa hands the cashier $30.00.)
CASHIER	Here is your dollar in change. Thank you and have a nice day.

21

Shopping V

Specific Foods

SHANNON	What's your favorite dairy product?
KAREN	My favorite dairy product is ice cream—chocolate ice cream. What's yours?
SHANNON	I like yogurt—peach yogurt.
SHANNON	What is your least favorite dairy product?
KAREN	My least favorite is sour cream. What is your least favorite dairy product?
SHANNON	Cottage cheese.
KAREN	I have an idea. Let's go to the ice cream store. I'll get an ice cream cone and you can get some frozen yogurt.
SHANNON	OK. Let's go!

(At the ice cream store)

SHANNON	Look at all the different flavors of ice cream and frozen yogurt!
KAREN	I think I'll get a double scoop of chocolate ice cream.
SHANNON	I think I'll get a double scoop of frozen peach yogurt.

(Shannon and Karen order their ice cream and yogurt and pay the cashier.)

KAREN	Let's come here again real soon!

SHANNON	What's your favorite dairy product?
KAREN	_____ _____
SHANNON	I like yogurt—peach yogurt.
SHANNON	_____
KAREN	My least favorite is sour cream. What is your least favorite dairy product?
SHANNON	Cottage cheese.
KAREN	I have an idea. Let's go to the ice cream store. I'll get an ice cream cone and you can get some frozen yogurt.
SHANNON	OK. Let's go!

(At the ice cream store)

SHANNON	Look at all the different flavors of ice cream and frozen yogurt!
KAREN	_____ _____
SHANNON	I think I'll get a double scoop of frozen peach yogurt.

(Shannon and Karen order their ice cream and yogurt and pay the cashier.)

KAREN	Let's come here again real soon!

22

Meals

TOMMY	What did you have for breakfast this morning?
TINA	I had hot cereal, hot tea, and a glass of orange juice. What did you have for breakfast, Tommy?
TOMMY	I had French toast with butter and syrup, bacon, sausage, and some hot chocolate.
TINA	Who sets the table and who washes the dishes after breakfast?
TOMMY	I clean the dishes and put them in the dishwasher. My sister sets the table and unloads the dishwasher after the dishes have been washed.
TINA	Who cooks breakfast for everyone?
TOMMY	We usually cook our own breakfast in the morning because everybody leaves the house at a different time. On the weekends, my mom or dad cooks a big breakfast for everyone.

TOMMY   What did you have _____?

TINA   _____

                 _____

TOMMY   I had _____

                 _____

TINA   Who sets the table and who washes the dishes after breakfast?

TOMMY   _____

                 _____

                 _____

                 _____

TINA   Who cooks_____?

TOMMY   _____

                 _____

                 _____

                 _____

                 _____

23

At the Restaurant

(Making a Reservation)

HOSTESS	Good evening. Hilltop Restaurant. May I help you?
ROSEMARY	Hello. I'd like to make a reservation for dinner tonight.
HOSTESS	How many in your party?
ROSEMARY	There are four of us.
HOSTESS	At what time would you like your reservation?
ROSEMARY	6:00.
HOSTESS	Can I have your name, please?
ROSEMARY	Rosemary St. Clair.
HOSTESS	OK. Your reservation is for a party of four at 6:00 for St. Clair. Thank you Ms. St. Clair.
ROSEMARY	Thank you and good-bye.

(Arriving at the Restaurant)

HOSTESS	Hello. May I help you?
ROSEMARY	Yes. I have a reservation for four at 6:00 for St. Clair.
HOSTESS	Yes, Ms. St. Clair. We have your reservation. Follow me, please.

(Ordering)

WAITER	Would you care for something to drink before dinner?
ROSEMARY	No, thank you. We'd like to see the menu, please.
WAITER	Of course. Here you are. Our special tonight is prime rib.
ROSEMARY	I'll take the prime rib, please. I'd like that cooked medium well.
WAITER	You have a choice of soup or salad. Which would you like?
ROSEMARY	Salad, please.
WAITER	What kind of dressing would you like on your salad?
ROSEMARY	Italian dressing, please. I would also like a cup of coffee with my dinner.

WAITER	Thank you. I'll be right back with your coffee and your salad.

(Paying the Bill)

WAITER	How was your dinner?
ROSEMARY	It was excellent, thank you.
WAITER	Will there be anything else?
ROSEMARY	Yes. May we please have the check?

(The waiter brings the check on a tray.)

WAITER	Here you are. Thank you and have a nice evening.
ROSEMARY	Thank you very much.

24

Sports and Sports Equipment

JUSTIN	Which sports are you good at playing?
RYAN	I'm good at baseball and basketball.
JUSTIN	What is your favorite "participant" sport?
RYAN	My favorite "participant" sport is baseball.
JUSTIN	Which position do you play in baseball?
RYAN	My favorite position is shortstop.
RYAN	What is your favorite "spectator" sport?
JUSTIN	My favorite "spectator" sport is football.
RYAN	Do you watch a lot of football?
JUSTIN	Yes. I watch it on TV and I also attend the games.
RYAN	Have you ever gone to a professional football game?
JUSTIN	Yes. I have season tickets to the New England Patriots' football games. I have been going to professional football games for ten years.
RYAN	Where do you go to see these games?
JUSTIN	I go to Gillette Stadium in the city of Foxborough, Massachusetts.
RYAN	Who is your favorite football player?
JUSTIN	My favorite football player is the quarterback for the Patriots, Tom Brady.

JUSTIN   Which sports are you good at playing?

RYAN   _____

JUSTIN   What is your favorite "participant" sport?

RYAN   _____

JUSTIN   Which position do you play in baseball?

RYAN   _____

RYAN   _____

JUSTIN   My favorite "spectator" sport is _____.

RYAN   Do you watch a lot of football?

JUSTIN   Yes. I watch it on TV and I also attend the games.

RYAN   Have you ever gone to a professional football game?

JUSTIN   _____

                    _____

                    _____

                    _____

RYAN   Where do you go to see these games?

JUSTIN   _____

RYAN   Who is your favorite _____?

JUSTIN   _____

                    _____

                    _____

                    _____

25

Feelings and Emotions

ALICE	Ashley, what's wrong? Why are you so sad and depressed?
ASHLEY	I didn't pass my English test.
ALICE	Did you study?
ASHLEY	No, I didn't. My parents are going to be angry with me.
ALICE	Do you think they will still let you go to the dance on Saturday night?
ASHLEY	I am certain that they won't let me go. They will be so disappointed with me. Next time I'm going to do the smart thing—STUDY!

(Alice tells her mother about the test.)

ASHLEY	I have something to tell you. I didn't pass my English test.
MOTHER	Why not? Didn't you study for the test?
ASHLEY	No. I didn't. I thought I could pass the test without studying. I was wrong.
MOTHER	I'm disappointed in you. You know you won't be able to go to the dance on Saturday.
ASHLEY	Yes, I know. From now on I am going to study hard before taking my exams.

ALICE   Ashley, what's wrong? Why are you so sad and depressed?

ASHLEY   _____.

ALICE   Did you study?

ASHLEY   _____

                        _____

ALICE   Do you think they will still let you go to the dance on Saturday night?

ASHLEY   _____

                        _____

                        _____

                        _____

(Alice tells her mother about the test.)

ASHLEY   I have something to tell you. I didn't pass my English test.

MOTHER   _____

ASHLEY   No. I didn't. I thought I could pass the test without studying. I was wrong.

MOTHER   _____

                        _____

                        _____

ASHLEY   Yes, I know. From now on I am going to study hard before taking my exams.

26

Leisure Time I

Hobbies, Activities, and Interests at Home

BRIAN	What do you like to do with your free time at home?
ANDY	I like to play basketball with my brother in front of our house.
BRIAN	Do you have any hobbies that you do at home?
ANDY	Yes, I do. I build model airplanes.
BRIAN	Do you sometimes watch TV when you have free time?
ANDY	Yes. I watch sports on TV and sometimes play Xbox.
BRIAN	What is your favorite Xbox game?
ANDY	I love to play Minecraft.
BRIAN	Does watching television help your English?
ANDY	It helps very much. I enjoy watching American television.

BRIAN   What do you like to do with your _____?

ANDY   I like to _____

_____

BRIAN   Do you have any _____?

ANDY   Yes, I do. I _____.

BRIAN   Do you sometimes watch TV when you have free time?

ANDY   _____

_____

_____

BRIAN   What is your favorite Xbox game?

ANDY   _____

BRIAN   Does watching television help your English?

ANDY   It helps very much. I enjoy watching American television.

Leisure Time II

Hobbies, Activities, and Interests Away from Home

LILY	What do you do with your free time away from home?
BELLA	I like to go shopping.
LILY	I love to go shopping! I especially like to go clothes shopping.
LILY	Have you ever been to a rock concert?
BELLA	No. I don't like rock concerts that much.
LILY	Have you ever gone on a picnic?
BELLA	Yes. My family and I go on picnics during the summer. They are a lot of fun. We usually picnic near a lake or at the beach.
LILY	What kind of food do you bring (pack) on a picnic?
BELLA	Sandwiches, fruit, drinks, chips, cookies, and sometimes, candy.
LILY	Do you like to picnic at the beach? Doesn't the sand get into your food?
BELLA	I love to picnic at the beach. Yes, sometimes the sand does get into the food.
LILY	What else do you do at the beach?
BELLA	I swim and body surf the waves.
LILY	This summer we should pack a picnic lunch and go to the beach!

LILY   What do you do with your _____ away from home?

BELLA   _____

LILY   I love to go shopping! I especially like to go _____

_____.

LILY (cont.) Have you ever been to a _____?

BELLA   _____

LILY   Have you ever gone on a picnic?

BELLA   _____

_____

_____

_____

LILY   What kind of food do you bring (pack) on a picnic?

BELLA   _____

_____

LILY   Do you like to picnic at the beach? Doesn't the sand get into your food?

BELLA   _____

_____

LILY   What else do you do at the beach?

BELLA   _____

_____

LILY   This summer we should pack a picnic lunch and go to the beach!

28

Living Quarters/Dwellings I

NANCY	Where do you live?
KATHY	I live in a condominium in Los Angeles.
NANCY	Does your family own or rent their condo?
KATHY	They own it.
NANCY	Do you like your neighborhood and your neighbors?
KATHY	Yes. It's a beautiful neighborhood and our neighbors are very friendly.
NANCY	How long have you lived here?
KATHY	I have lived there two years now.
NANCY	Where were you born?
KATHY	I was born in Acapulco. I came to the United States five years ago.
NANCY	How do you like living in the United States?
KATHY	I like it very much. I'm glad I live here.

NANCY   Where do you live?

KATHY   _____

               _____

NANCY   _____

               _____

KATHY   They own it.

NANCY   Do you like your neighborhood and your neighbors?

KATHY   _____

               _____

               _____

NANCY   _____

KATHY   I have lived there two years now.

NANCY   Where were you born?

KATHY   _____

               _____

               _____

NANCY   How do you like living in the United States?

KATHY   _____

29

Living Quarters/Dwellings II

BRITTANY	Do you own or rent your house?
MOLLY	I own it.
BRITTANY	How many rooms are there in your house?
MOLLY	I have four bedrooms and two bathrooms.
BRITTANY	Do you have a backyard?
MOLLY	Yes. I have a large backyard with a swimming pool.
BRITTANY	Do you have a separate laundry room?
MOLLY	No. My washer and dryer are in the garage.
MOLLY	Where do you live, Brittany?
BRITTANY	I live in a condo. It's a one-story dwelling. I really like it.
MOLLY	How many rooms do you have?
BRITTANY	It has two bedrooms, one bathroom, and a small patio. The complex also has a gym, swimming pool, and hot tub.
MOLLY	Do you rent or own your condo?
BRITTANY	I rent it.

BRITTANY   _____?

MOLLY   I own it.

BRITTANY   How many rooms are there in your house?

MOLLY   _____

BRITTANY   Do you have a backyard?

MOLLY   _____.

BRITTANY   Do you have a separate laundry room?

MOLLY   _____.

MOLLY   Where do you live, Brittany?

BRITTANY   _____

     _____

MOLLY   How many rooms do you have?

BRITTANY   _____

     _____

     _____

MOLLY   Do you rent or own your condo?

BRITTANY   _____

30

Rooms in the Home I

Living Room, Dining Room, Hall, and Corridor

DEBBIE	Do you spend much time in your living room?
JOEY	Yes. That's where I watch TV and play video games.
DEBBIE	Is there a fireplace in your living room?
JOEY	Yes. There is a large, brick fireplace in there. It keeps the room very warm.
DEBBIE	Does your family eat in the dining room very often?
JOEY	No. We eat in there only when we have guests for dinner or for a special occasion. Next week is my grandmother's birthday. My whole family will be here to celebrate it. We will be eating dinner in the dining room that evening.

DEBBIE   Do you spend much time in your living room?

JOEY   _____

            _____

            _____

            _____

DEBBIE   Is there a fireplace in your living room?

JOEY   _____

            _____

            _____

DEBBIE   Does your family eat in the dining room very often?

JOEY   _____

            _____

            _____

            _____

            _____

            _____

            _____

            _____

            _____

31

Rooms in the Home II

The Kitchen

MAYA	Is your kitchen big or small?
ISABEL	I have a big kitchen.
MAYA	Do you have an eating area in your kitchen?
ISABEL	I have an eating area with a table and four chairs, and also a counter with four bar stools.
MAYA	What appliances do you have in your kitchen?
ISABEL	I have a self-cleaning, double oven, a microwave, a dishwasher, a trash compacter, a refrigerator and freezer that also has an ice maker, a food processor, an electric can opener, and a coffee maker.
MAYA	Your kitchen sounds beautiful!

MAYA   Is your kitchen _____?

ISABEL   I have a _____

MAYA   Do you have a _____ in your kitchen?

ISABEL   _____

       _____

       _____

       _____

MAYA   What appliances do you have in your kitchen?

ISABEL   _____

       _____

       _____

       _____

       _____

       _____

       _____

MAYA   Your kitchen sounds _____!

32

Rooms in the Home III

The Bedroom

KRIS	How many bedrooms are there in your house?
KATHY	There are four bedrooms.
KRIS	Does anyone share a bedroom?
KATHY	No. Each of us has our own bedroom.
KRIS	Do you make everyone's bed each day?
KATHY	Sometimes, but usually everyone makes their own bed.
KRIS	Do your children take care of their own bedrooms?
KATHY	Most of the time. They are supposed to put away their clothes, make the bed, and keep their rooms neat and clean.
KRIS	What size is your bed? What size are your children's beds?
KATHY	My bed is a king-size, my son has a bunk bed, and my daughter has a single, canopy bed.

KRIS   How many bedrooms are there in your house?

KATHY   _____

KRIS   _____?

KATHY   No. Each of us has our own bedroom.

KRIS   Do you make everyone's bed each day?

KATHY   _____

_____

KRIS   Do your children take care of their own bedrooms?

KATHY   _____

_____

_____

_____

_____

KRIS   What size is your bed? What size are your children's beds?

KATHY   _____

_____

_____

_____

33

Rooms in the Home IV

The Bathroom

RICK	How many bathrooms are there in your home?
STEVE	There are two and a half. There are two upstairs and one downstairs.
RICK	Do you have your own bathroom, or do you share a bathroom with another family member?
STEVE	My sister and I share one bathroom and my parents share the master bathroom.
RICK	Where is the half-bathroom located?
STEVE	It is located next to the den. It's also used as a guest bathroom.

RICK   How many bathrooms are there in your home?

STEVE   _____

_____

RICK   Do you have your own bathroom, or do you share a bathroom with another family member?

STEVE   _____

_____

_____

_____

RICK   Where is the half-bathroom located?

STEVE   _____

_____

_____

34

Household Chores and Home Maintenance

JANE	Do you have to do a lot of chores at home?
SALLY	Yes. I have quite a few chores to do every day.
JANE	What do you have to do?
SALLY	Every day, I have to make my bed, put all my clothes away, and clean my room. When I come home from school, I have to empty the dishwasher and put all the dishes, silverware, and glasses where they belong.
JANE	Do you have any weekend chores?
SALLY	I have to vacuum the rugs and polish the glass tables in the living room.
JANE	What does your brother do?
SALLY	He mows the lawn, feeds the dog, cat, bird, and hamster and takes out the garbage. He also has to make his bed and clean his room. Both my mom and dad work during the week, so my brother and I have to help them by doing our chores.
JANE	Who sets the table?
SALLY	We both do. One night I set the table and the next night my brother sets the table.
JANE	Do you ever babysit?
SALLY	Yes. I babysit on weekends. I make a lot of money babysitting.
JANE	Do you and your brother get an allowance?
SALLY	Yes. My parents give us an allowance for helping with the household chores.

JANE   Do you have to do a lot of chores at home?

SALLY   _____.

JANE   What do you have to do?

SALLY   _____

             _____

             _____

             _____

JANE   Do you have any weekend chores?

SALLY   _____

             _____

JANE   What does your brother do?

SALLY   _____

             _____

             _____

             _____

JANE   Who sets the table?

SALLY   _____

             _____

JANE   Do you ever babysit?

SALLY   _____

             _____.

JANE   Do you and your brother get an allowance?

SALLY   _____

             _____

35

The Post Office

TERESA	Where are you going with all those packages, Sarah?
SARAH	I'm going to the post office.
TERESA	Which one—the one on Grant Avenue or the one on Center Road?
SARAH	The post office on Center Road. I'm sending birthday gifts to my niece and nephew in New Orleans, Louisiana.
TERESA	How will you send them? Are you going to insure them?
SARAH	I am going to send them first-class insured. It's always better to insure your packages in case they get lost or stolen.
TERESA	Could you do me a favor when you get to the post office?
SARAH	Sure. What would you like for me to do?
TERESA	Could you get me a roll of stamps? Here's the money.
SARAH	I'll bring you the stamps this afternoon. See you then.
TERESA	Bye, Sarah, and thanks!

TERESA   _____?

SARAH   I'm going to the post office.

TERESA   Which one—the one on _____ or the one on _____?

SARAH   The post office on _____. I'm sending birthday gifts to my niece and
nephew in _____.

TERESA   How will you send them? Are you going to insure them?

SARAH   _____

                   _____

                   _____

TERESA   Could you do me a favor when you get to the post office?

SARAH   Sure. What would you like for me to do?

TERESA   Could you get me a roll of _____? Here's the money.

SARAH   I'll bring you the stamps this afternoon. See you then.

TERESA   _____!

36

Time, the Calendar, Holidays, and Celebrations

JOHNNIE	What's the date today?
RICHIE	Today is March 12.
JOHNNIE	What day is St. Patrick's Day?
RICHIE	It is Friday, March 17. Why?
JOHNNIE	There is going to be a big St. Patrick's Day celebration and parade in downtown. It starts at noon. I really want to go. Why don't you come with me?
RICHIE	I would love to! Thanks for asking me.
RICHIE	What are your favorite holidays?
JOHNNIE	Besides St. Patrick's Day, I like New Year's Eve, Christmas, Easter, and Halloween.
RICHIE	Those holidays are my favorites, too. On New Year's Eve, I like to go to out to dinner with my family and ring in the new year. On Christmas, I like to give and receive presents. I also get to spend a lot of time with my family and friends. Easter is fun because I like to color Easter eggs with my younger brother. On Halloween I can be anyone I want. Dressing up in costumes is a lot of fun. I really enjoy the holidays and their customs.

JOHNNIE   What's the date today?

RICHIE   _____

JOHNNIE   What day is St. Patrick's Day?

RICHIE   It is Friday, March 17. Why?

JOHNNIE   _____

                  _____

                  _____

RICHIE   I would love to! Thanks for asking me.

RICHIE   _____

JOHNNIE   Besides St. Patrick's Day, I like _____

                  _____

RICHIE   _____

                  _____

                  _____

                  _____

                  _____

                  _____

37

Weather and Seasons

ANNA   Should I take a coat to school today? The weather outside looks cold.

JOANN   The weatherman said that is was going to be foggy and chilly this morning, but that it would clear up this afternoon. It's supposed to be a nice day.

ANNA   I wish it would snow. I want to go snowboarding, but there is very little snow in the mountains. All the snow is melting. The weather is too warm for this time of the year. Winter should be very cold and have a lot of snow. If it doesn't snow soon, we may have a drought.

JOANN   I heard that there are tornados and hurricanes in the south and flash flood warnings in the east.

ANNA   All I care about, right now, is the west. I just wish it would snow!

JOANN   Which season do you like the best?

ANNA   I like summer the best. The weather is hot and I can go to the beach and surf. Which season do you like the best?

JOANN   I like summer because we're out of school. I like spring because the weather is warm and everything is in bloom. I like winter because I can go snowboarding and I like autumn because the leaves have changed into such beautiful colors. I guess *all* the seasons are my favorites!

ANNA   Should I take a coat to school today? The weather outside looks cold.

JOANN   _____

                     _____

                     _____

                     _____

ANNA   I wish it would snow. I want to go _____ but there is very little snow in the mountains. All the snow is _____. The weather is too _____ for this time of the year. Winter should be very _____ and have a lot of _____. If it doesn't snow soon, we may have a _____.

JOANN   I heard that there are tornados and hurricanes in the south and flash flood warnings in the east.

ANNA   _____

                     _____

JOANN   Which season do you like the best?

ANNA   _____

                     _____

                     _____

                     _____

JOANN   I like summer because we're _____. I like spring because the weather is _____ and everything is in bloom. I like winter because I can go _____ and I like autumn because the leaves have changed into such beautiful _____. I guess *all* the seasons are my favorites!

38

Transportation I

By Road

BRIAN	I'm so excited! Today I am going to buy my dream car.
ANDRE	What kind of car are you going to buy?
BRIAN	It's a 1970 Ford Mustang. It's beautiful!
ANDRE	Which model is it?
BRIAN	It's a Mach I.
ANDRE	Is it stock?
BRIAN	Yes. Everything in it is original.
ANDRE	Are you going to change the interior or exterior?
BRIAN	The only thing I am changing are the tires. I can't change anything else or it will no longer be in stock condition.
ANDRE	How much will your insurance cost?
BRIAN	It will cost me $800 a year. I'm working twenty hours a week to pay for insurance, gas, and any repairs the car may need.
ANDRE	The car sounds great! Bring it by after you buy it. We'll go for a ride.
BRIAN	OK! See you later.

BRIAN   I'm so excited! Today I am going to buy my dream car.

ANDRE   What kind of car are you going to buy?

BRIAN   _____

                       _____

ANDRE   Which model is it?

BRIAN   _____

                       _____

ANDRE   Is it stock?

BRIAN   Yes. Everything in it is original.

ANDRE   Are you going to change the interior or exterior?

BRIAN   _____

                       _____

ANDRE   How much will your insurance cost?

BRIAN   _____

                       _____

                       _____

                       _____

ANDRE   The car sounds great! Bring it by after you buy it. We'll go for a ride.

BRIAN   _____

39

Transportation II

Public Transportation

BRITT	I'm going shopping in San Francisco today. I'm going to take the cable car.
NOEL	Can I come with you? I love to ride on the cable car.
BRITT	Sure, you can come. I don't know how those cable cars can go up and down those steep hills!
NOEL	What kind of public transportation will we take to the city?
BRITT	We'll have to take the transit bus from here and transfer to the local bus that stops at the Golden Gate Bridge bus stop. That bus will take us to San Francisco.
NOEL	Let's not forget to get our bus transfers from the bus driver.
BRITT	I have two extra tickets for the transit bus. Here, I'll give you one.
NOEL	Thanks, Britt!
BRITT	Well, let's go. I don't want to miss the bus. The bus schedule says it leaves every hour on the hour. Hurry!

BRITT   I'm going shopping in _____ today. I'm going to take the cable car.

NOEL   _____

_____

BRITT   Sure, you can come. I don't know how those cable cars can go up and down those _____!

NOEL   What kind of public transportation will we take to the city?

BRITT   _____

_____

_____

_____

_____

_____

_____

_____

NOEL   Let's not forget to get our _____ from the bus driver.

BRITT   I have two extra _____ for the transit bus. Here, I'll give you one.

NOEL   Thanks, Britt!

BRITT   Well, let's go. I don't want to miss the bus. The bus schedule says it leaves every hour on the hour. Hurry!

40

Transportation III

Alternatives by Road

RYAN	How do you get to school every morning?
CAMERON	I usually ride my bike or my scooter to school. If the weather is nice, I walk.
RYAN	How do you get to school when it rains?
CAMERON	My mom drives me.
RYAN	How did you get to school this morning? Did you ride your bike?
CAMERON	No. My bike has a flat tire, the brakes aren't working very well, and the chain fell off. I rode my scooter to school this morning.
RYAN	What color is your scooter?
CAMERON	It's silver and black. It has handbrakes and a kickstand.
RYAN	I heard that your brother, Justin, bought a motor scooter. Is it true?
CAMERON	Yes. He bought a red and black Honda scooter. It's really nice.
RYAN	Do your mom and dad like the scooter?
CAMERON	Yes, but they told him that he must wear a helmet and obey all the traffic laws. They want him to be very careful or they will not let him ride the motor scooter.
RYAN	I think they are dangerous. I saw an accident involving a motorcycle and a car. The ambulance came and put the motorcyclist on a stretcher. They took him to the hospital.
CAMERON	I hope that my brother is very careful when riding his scooter.

RYAN   How do you get to school every morning?

CAMERON   _____

                   _____

RYAN   How do you get to school when it rains?

CAMERON   _____

RYAN   How did you get to school this morning? Did you ride your bike?

CAMERON   _____

                   _____

RYAN   What color is your _____?

CAMERON   _____

                   _____

                   _____.

RYAN   I heard that your brother bought a _____. Is it true?

CAMERON   Yes. He bought a _____. It's really nice.

RYAN   Do your mom and dad like the _____?

CAMERON   _____

                   _____

                   _____

RYAN   I think they are dangerous. I saw an accident involving a motorcycle and a car. The ambulance came and put the motorcyclist on a stretcher. They took him to the hospital.

CAMERON   _____

                   _____

41

Transportation IV

The Train

JEFF	Have you ever ridden on a train?
MIKE	Yes. It was fun.
JEFF	Where did you go?
MIKE	I took a train from Los Angeles, California, and went to New York City, New York.
JEFF	How long did it take?
MIKE	It took three days.
JEFF	What did you do on the train?
MIKE	My family and I slept in the sleeping car and we ate in the dining car. I read a little and played cards with my older sister. We also brought along some board games.
JEFF	Did you enjoy the trip?
MIKE	Yes, I enjoyed the trip very much! I'd like to take another train trip soon.

JEFF   Have you ever ridden on a train?

MIKE   _____

JEFF   Where did you go?

MIKE   _____

      _____

JEFF   How long did it take?

MIKE   _____

JEFF   What did you do on the train?

MIKE   _____

      _____

      _____

      _____

      _____

JEFF   Did you enjoy the trip?

MIKE   _____

      _____

42

Transportation V

By Air

MARK	Do you like to travel in airplanes?
MONTE	I love to fly. I especially like to fly in a 747. Do you like to fly?
MARK	No. I don't like to fly. I get airsick.
MONTE	Did you know that Larry's dad has his own plane?
MARK	No, I didn't. Does he fly it often?
MONTE	He flies his plane every weekend.
MARK	My mom made airline reservations for Disneyland, but I'm afraid the plane might crash.
MONTE	Don't worry, Mark. Everything will be fine. Make sure you sit in an aisle seat and bring your DVD player so you can watch a movie. The flight is short, so you won't be in the air that long.
MARK	We're leaving Sunday, the 10th, and coming home Thursday, the 14th. It's all been confirmed.
MONTE	Have a great time, Mark and say "Hi" to Mickey Mouse for me!

MARK   Do you like to travel in airplanes?

MONTE   _____

                           _____

MARK   No. I don't like to fly. I get airsick.

MONTE   Did you know that Larry's dad has his own plane?

MARK   _____

MONTE   He flies his plane every weekend.

MARK   My mom made airline reservations for _____

                           _____

MONTE   Don't worry, Mark. Everything will be fine. Make sure you sit in an aisle seat and bring your _____. The flight is _____ so you won't be in the _____ that long.

MARK   We're leaving _____ and coming home _____. It's all been _____.

MONTE   Have a great time, Mark and say "Hi" to _____ for me!

43

Transportation VI

By Water

VICKI	Have you ever traveled by ship?
MARK	Yes. I took a cruise last year.
VICKI	Where did you go?
MARK	I went to Mexico. We docked at Puerto Vaillarta, Mazatlan, and Cabo San Lucas.
VICKI	That sounds like a lot of fun. Did you enjoy it?
MARK	Yes, especially the food! I also had a beautiful stateroom with a porthole window.
VICKI	Have you ever rowed in a rowboat or paddled in a canoe?
MARK	Only once and it was in a canoe. It was too much work. I'd rather cruise around on a cruise ship.
VICKI	I think I'll talk to my travel agent. A cruise sounds like a great idea!

VICKI   Have you ever traveled by ship?

MARK   _____

VICKI   Where did you go?

MARK   _____

        _____

        _____

VICKI   That sounds like a lot of fun. Did you enjoy it?

MARK   _____

        _____

        _____

VICKI   Have you ever rowed in a rowboat or paddled in a canoe?

MARK   _____

        _____

VICKI   I think I'll talk to my _____.

        A cruise sounds like a great idea!

44

Taking a Vacation/Trip

BONNIE — How many trips did you go on this year?

TOMAS — I went on four. Two were vacation trips and two were business trips.

BONNIE — Where did you go on your vacation this year?

TOMAS — First, I went to Miami, Florida. The weather was very hot and I spent most of the day at the beach. Next, I went to Hollywood, California. I was given a guided tour of Universal Studios. That's where they make movies. It was very interesting and a lot of fun.

BONNIE — That sounds great! Where did you go for your business trips?

TOMAS — I flew to New York City and stayed at the beautiful and very expensive Waldorf-Astoria Hotel for two days. Then I took a train to Wilmington, Delaware. I rented a car while I was there. I wish I could have stayed longer in Delaware. It's such a beautiful state. Did you go anywhere this year, Bonnie?

BONNIE — I did a lot of skiing and snowboarding this winter. I snowboarded at Squaw Valley, California, and Sun Valley, Idaho. In Aspen, Colorado, I skied. It was wonderful! My parents have a time-share vacation plan. I always have a condo ready when I want to go skiing.

TOMAS — You're really lucky! Do you buy a lot of souvenirs when you travel?

BONNIE — I buy t-shirts with names of the ski resorts where I ski. I take a lot of photos, too.

TOMAS — You will have to show me the photos of your ski vacations. I would very much like to see them.

BONNIE — Sure. Let's get together soon.

TOMAS — I'll call you next week, OK?

BONNIE — Sounds good! See you later. Bye, Tomas.

TOMAS — Bye, Bonnie.

BONNIE   How many trips did you go on this year?

TOMAS   _____

                _____

BONNIE   Where did you go on your vacation this year?

TOMAS   _____

                _____

                _____

                _____

                _____

                _____

                _____

BONNIE   That sounds great! Where did you go for your business trips?

TOMAS   _____

                _____

                _____

                _____

                _____

                _____

                _____

                _____

BONNIE   I did a lot of _____ this winter. I snowboarded at Squaw Valley, California, and Sun Valley, Idaho. In Aspen, Colorado, I skied. It was wonderful! My parents have a _____ vacation plan. I always have a _____ ready when I want to go _____.

TOMAS   You're really lucky! Do you buy a lot of _____ when you travel?

BONNIE   _____

                _____

                _____

                _____

TOMAS   You will have to show me the _____ of your _____. I would very much like to see them.

BONNIE   _____

BONNIE   Sounds good! See you later. Bye, Tomas.

TOMAS   Bye, Bonnie.

About the Author

University of San Francisco graduate and author Dr. **Kristine Setting Clark** was a long-time feature writer for the San Francisco 49ers' and Dallas Cowboys' *Gameday* Magazine. A gifted athlete in her own right, physical education teacher, wife, mother, and later, a high school administrator and college professor, Dr. Clark has never let anything stand in the way of her goals; not even a life-threatening bout with Hodgkin's Disease, blindness in both eyes for ten months, and the resulting partial blindness, at age twenty-six. Her passion for life, her incredible optimism, and her drive to live life to the fullest has endeared her to her former students, friends, and to those on whom she's written, including her childhood football idol and close friend, Bob St. Clair of the San Francisco 49ers.

Besides *Undefeated, Untied, and Uninvited: A Documentary of the 1951 University of San Francisco Dons' Football Team*, she has authored nine other books: *Legends of the Hall: 1950s; St Clair: I'll Take It Raw: The Life of Former San Francisco 49er and Hall of Fame Member, Bob St. Clair* (foreword by Gino Marchetti); *Lilly: A Cowboy's Story—The Life of Former Dallas Cowboys and Hall of Fame Member, Bob Lilly* (foreword by Roger Staubach); *Tittle: Nothing Comes Easy—The Life of Former Football Great and Hall of Fame Member, Y. A. Tittle* (foreword by Frank Gifford); *The Fire Within: The Life of Former Green Bay Packer and Hall of Fame Member, Jim Taylor* (foreword by Bart Starr); and *Controlled Violence: The Life of Former New York Giant, Washington Redskins, and Hall of Fame Member, Sam Huff* (foreword by Frank Gifford).

Released in July 2014 is her latest book, *The Fighting Donovans: A Family History of World Boxing Champion and Hall of Fame Boxer, Mike Donovan, World Champion Boxing Referee and Boxing Hall of Fame Referee Arthur Donovan, Sr. and former Baltimore Colt Defensive Tackle and Pro Football Hall of Fame Member, Arthur Donovan, Jr.* In the summer of 2016 her book on *Football's Fabulous Fifties: When Men Were Men and the Grass Was Still Real*, will be released by St. Johann's Press.

Her book *Cheating Is Encouraged!* with former Raider wide receiver Mike Siani was released through Skyhorse Publishing (an imprint of W.W. Norton) in September 2015. In December 2015 her memoirs on defeating cancer and blindness were published by Amazon. The book is titled *Death Was Never an Option! A Humorously Serious Story on Defeating Cancer and Blindness*.

Over the years, she has also held a number of book-signing events with the many celebrities from her books at the Pro Football Hall of Fame in Canton, Ohio. She has also been a keynote speaker for many corporate, sports, and educational venues. Clark is also an avid advisory board representative for Mike Ditka's Gridiron Greats Assistance Fund. In November 2014, Clark and the Santa Clara Chamber of Commerce officially kicked off their First Annual Chamber of Commerce/49ers/Gridiron Greats luncheon.

Dr. Clark's personality, close relationships with the subjects of her books, and engaging writing style allow her to reach the subject matter on a deeper level, taking the reader to otherwise unavailable territory: the sometimes humorous, always intriguing backstory of the famous events and players in the world of sports. In addition, her achievements have led to being a guest author on major sports talk radio shows. In February 2014, Clark's first book, *Undefeated Untied and Uninvited* was the subject of an ESPN documentary for Black History Month. The documentary, *The '51 Dons*, and was narrated by Johnny Mathis. She is currently working on a treatment for a documentary on her latest book, *The Fighting Donovans*.

In 1977 Clark was diagnosed with Stage IV Hodgkin's Disease and was given three months to live. She eventually beat the disease after enduring ten months of blindness caused by the grueling chemotherapy treatments. Her latest book, an autobiographical memoir, *Death Was Never An Option! A Humorously Serious Story on Beating Cancer* was released in December 2015.

Dr. Clark resides in Stockton, California, has two grown children and four grandsons. Her oldest grandson, Justin, is the godson of former All-Pro 49er and Hall of Fame member Bob St. Clair.